SUNDAY FOOTBALL

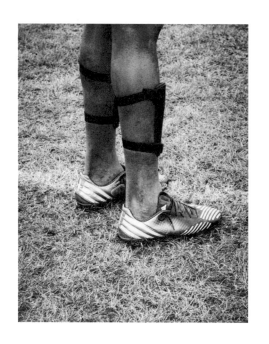

SUNDAY FOOTBALL

by Chris Baker

HOXTON MINI PRESS

To order books, collector's editions and signed prints go to:

www.hoxtonminipress.com

East London Photo Stories

Book Ten

FOREWORD

Hackney Marshes is legendary. Just ask David Beckham and Ian Wright. But in addition to the occasional famous face it's a special place for so many more. I love the fact that thousands of amateur footballers still turn up every week - whatever the weather - and do battle for 90 minutes. I love the fact that a huge variation of 'athletes' still change on the sidelines, have a cheeky fag before the game and will put their all into a game watched by a handful of hardy souls.

Chris Baker has done something very special with 'Sunday Football'. He's managed to capture the essence of football reminding us all of the reasons why we have so much affection for the beautiful game.

Dan Walker,
BBC Presenter, *Football Focus* and *Match of the Day*.

PHOTOGRAPHER'S NOTE

As a kid growing up in rural England, all I did was play football every waking moment for every team possible, all the while dreaming of one day being a professional. When I got to the age of around sixteen or seventeen I had trials for a couple of professional clubs that didn't work out. The dream fell away, and with it my love of football, until several years later when I discovered adult Sunday League. All of sudden football was back to being playground football: hanging out with mates, having a laugh, and if you won, great, if you didn't, who cared?! One player told me, "My wife doesn't get it, this is my social life, this is where I come to hang out with my mates!"

Amongst those mates there's always the guy turning up late, smoking a fag and stinking of booze; there's the flamboyant striker who refuses to pass and still shoots a mile wide (me); the guy who loses his temper at the drop of a hat; the stoic defender; the guy who's so unfit he either gets substituted before half time or gets ten minutes at the end of the game, and then there's the poor referee who would have a hard time controlling his dog let alone twenty-two amateur players kicking lumps out of each other. It was an obvious fit for my new project.

I'd wake up on Sunday morning, see the weather and know the type of shots I'd get. If it was raining, the teams would be light on players turning up, there would be horrible tackles flying around and some great portraits to be taken at the end of the games. If it was sunny, the fags and spliffs would be out and the sidelines would look like a hangover recovery clinic with players lying around looking like they'd barely be able to get up off the floor, let alone run around a pitch for forty-five minutes.

Hackney Marshes has a wonderfully rich footballing history. In 1947, with the recent backdrop of the war, the Hackney and Leyton Sunday League was formed, the pitches being built on the foundations of rubble created by the Blitz. Within ten years, football on the marshes was so popular it had become London's biggest sporting ground. Up to 2000 players would turn up on a Sunday morning, needing to book one of over 120 pitches up to ten months in advance. Hackney Marshes had begun it's ascendancy into footballing history.

But that's the history, not why I came to know it. For me, it was the mythical football place that I'd heard stories of, and not necessarily positive ones! Stories of regular fights and all kinds of broken bones caused by the terrible state of the pitches reached me. Adverts from huge sports companies occasionally aired on TV, featuring pitches as far as the eye could see. Ian Wright had played there, and then David Beckham, and no doubt countless other people on their way to professional status. And no matter where you lived in the country, if you played Sunday football, you'd heard of The Marshes, so where better to shoot a project on amateur football?

Sunday Football is my love letter to the game that consumed me for so many years. A visual interpretation of the beloved game at amateur level. An ode to those players that turn up late, hungover and discussing last night's conquest. Those who light a cigarette at half time whilst sucking an orange quarter for the supposed energy it gives you. Those that repeatedly call the referee, their team mates and the opposing team a 'cunt'. Those that get lost in the emotion of the game and start the occasional brawl on the pitch, and those that round off the weekend with a quick pint of beer with their teammates post-game before heading back to the missus and kids for a roast dinner... British Sunday league football at its best, every week of the season come rain or shine, at Hackney Marshes, the spiritual home of amateur football.

Chris Baker,
East London, 2016.

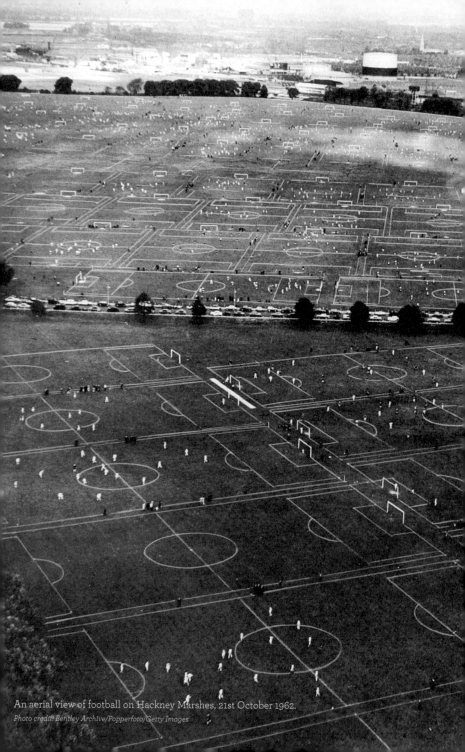

An aerial view of football on Hackney Marshes, 21st October 1962.
Photo credit: Bentley Archive/Popperfoto/Getty Images

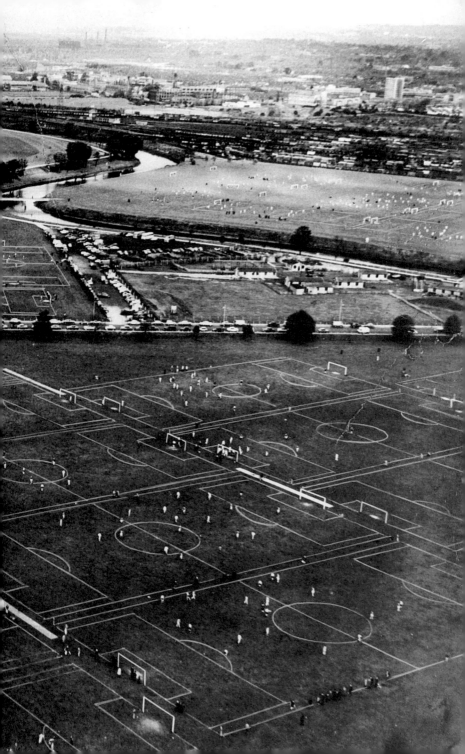

CHRIS BAKER

Chris Baker is a documentary and portrait photographer from London with a long history in the amateur game. After one too many injuries, Baker decided to get on the safe side of the sidelines and begin a two-year documentation of football on the Hackney Marshes. Prior to his obsession with photography, he worked for an independent record label.

HOXTON MINI PRESS

Hoxton Mini Press is the smallest imaginable publisher in East London and is run by Martin, a fine art photographer and Ann, who has worked in galleries for many years. They are dedicated to bringing photobooks to a much wider audience and think that as the whole world goes online beautiful books should be cherished. Feel free to stroke or smell this book. They have two dogs, Moose and Bug, who hate art.

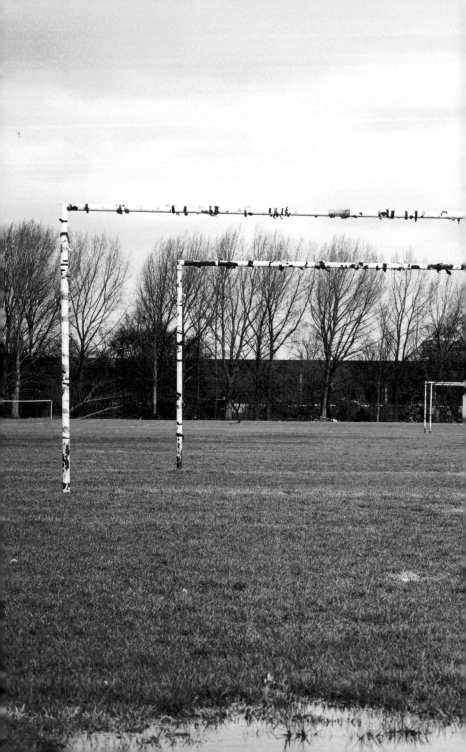

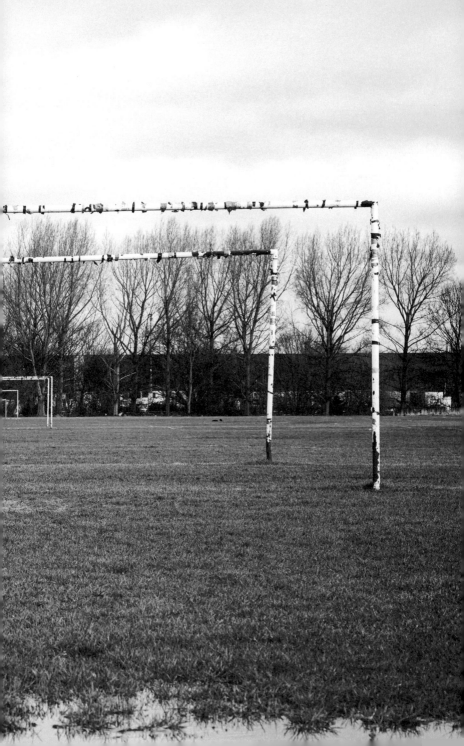

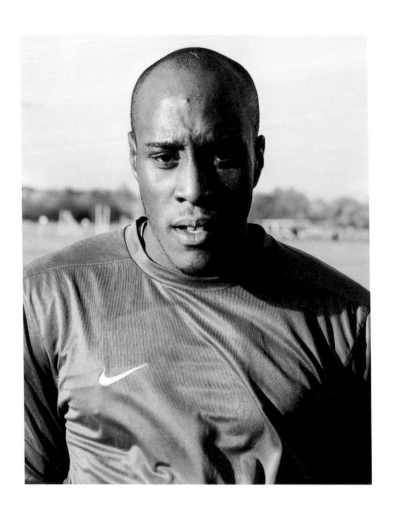

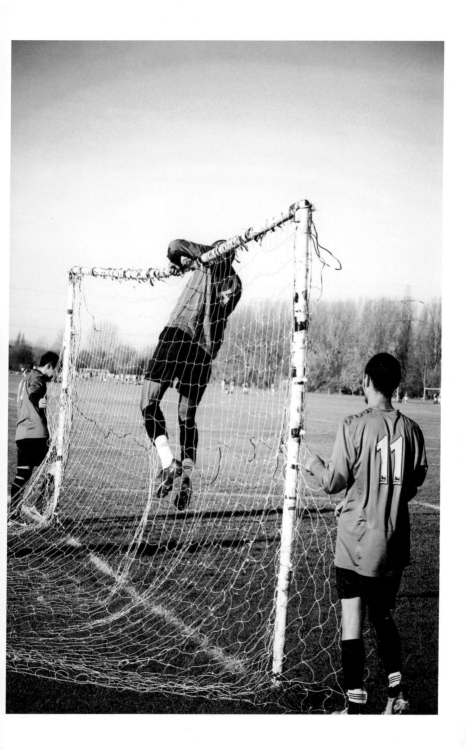

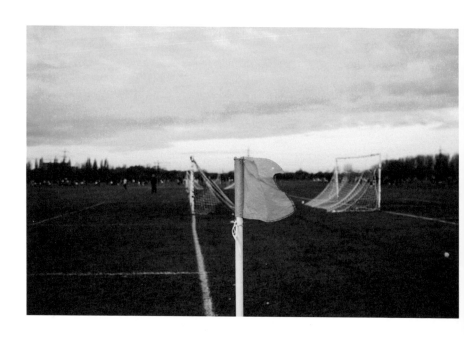

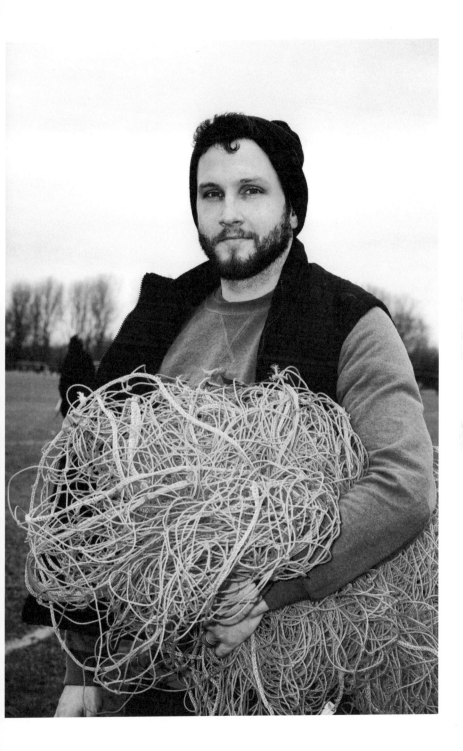

"Football is a family tied together in knowledge and passion, where everything comes together for ninety minutes, where everything else is second to playing football."

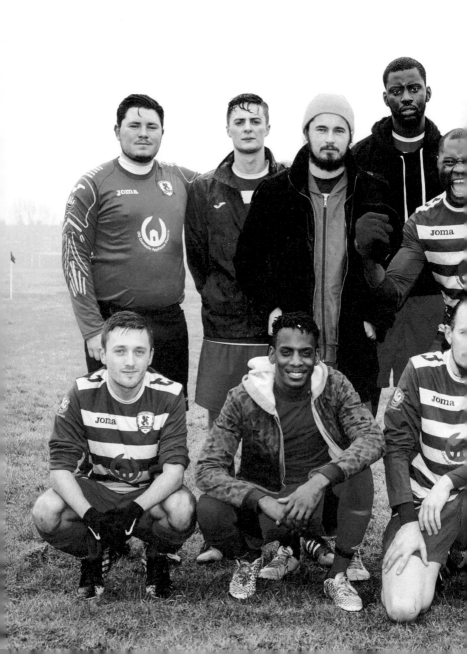

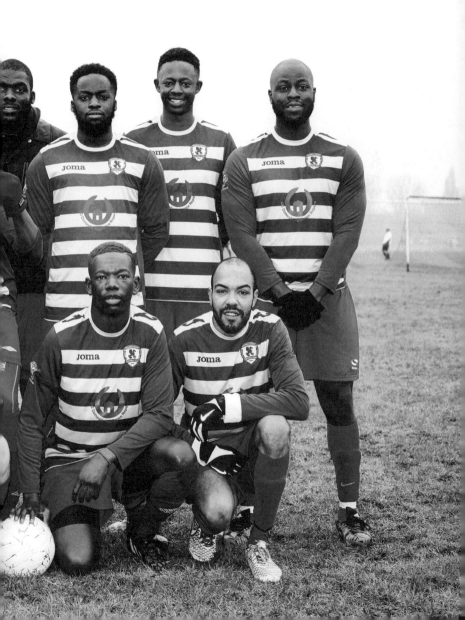

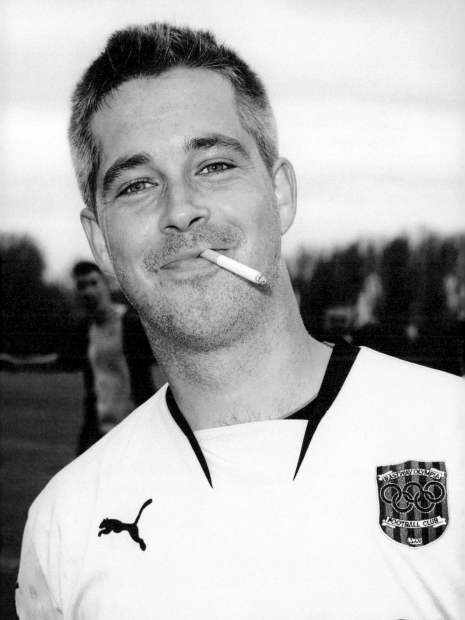

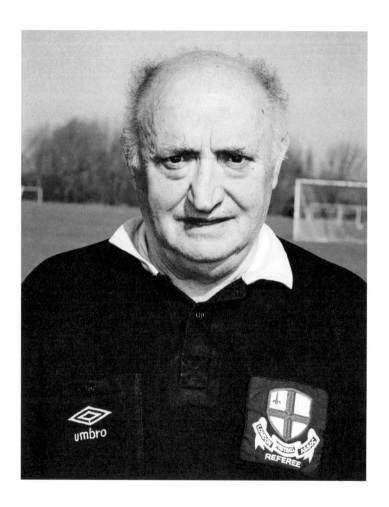

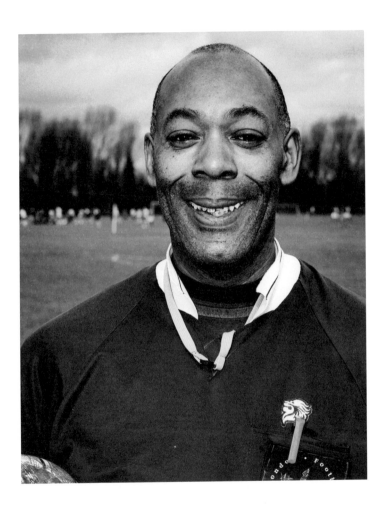

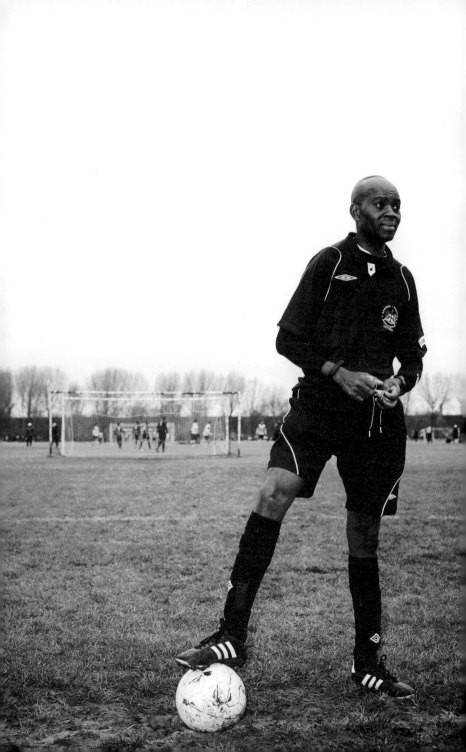

"I've refereed four hundred games and only had to abandon four: one for being head-butted, one for being pushed over, one after having sent a player off and him stating he was going to stay on after the game and knock me out, and the final one because a team kept fighting amongst themselves. Four in four hundred... not bad."

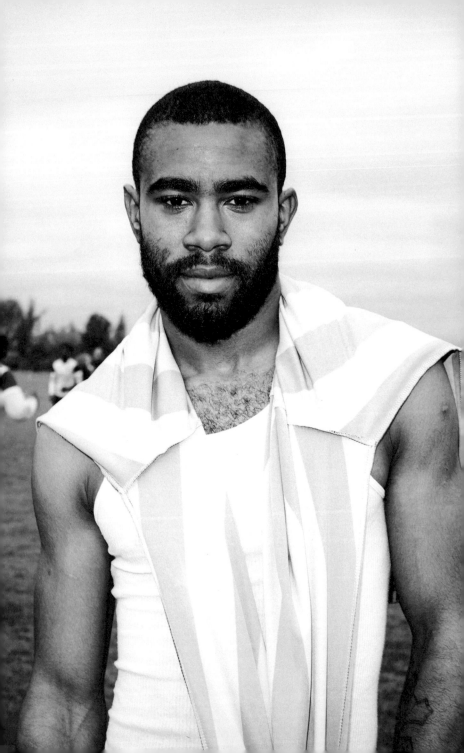

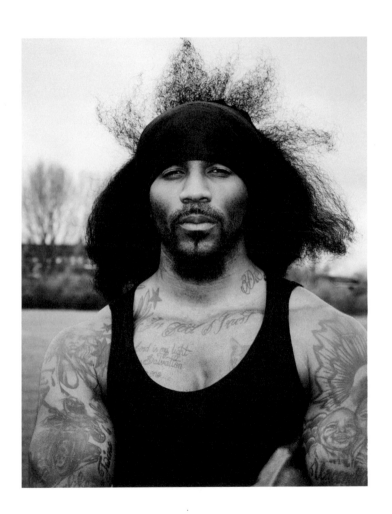

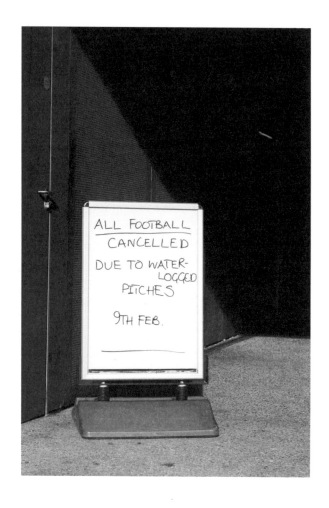

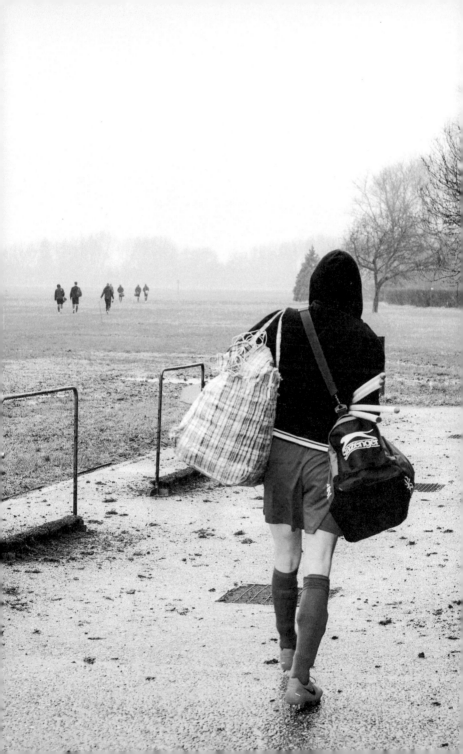

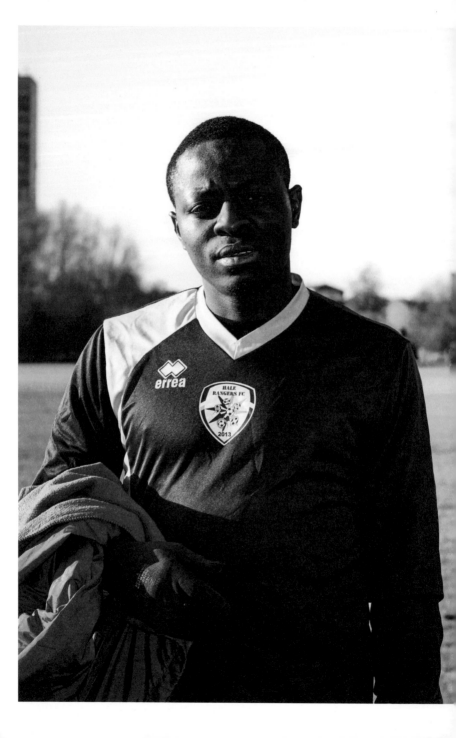

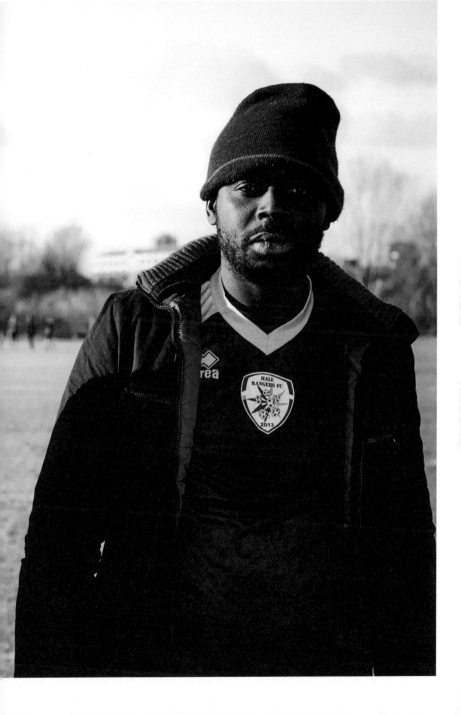

"Steven is still at his house?!?"

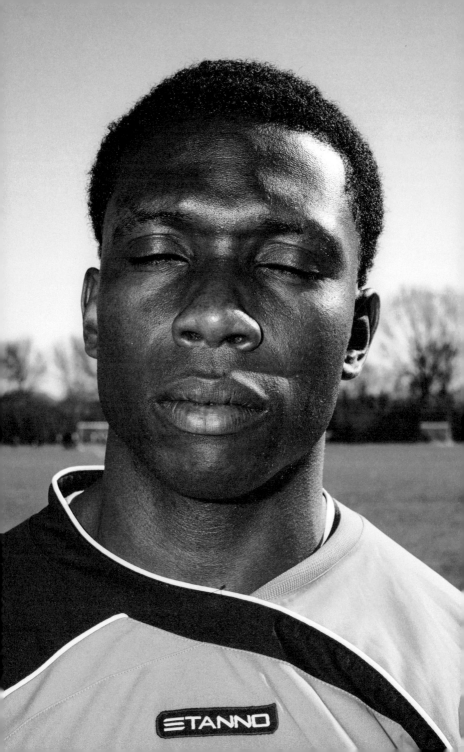

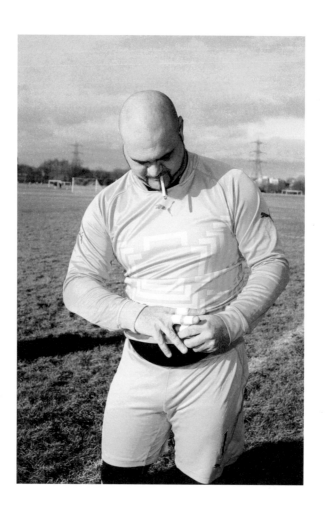

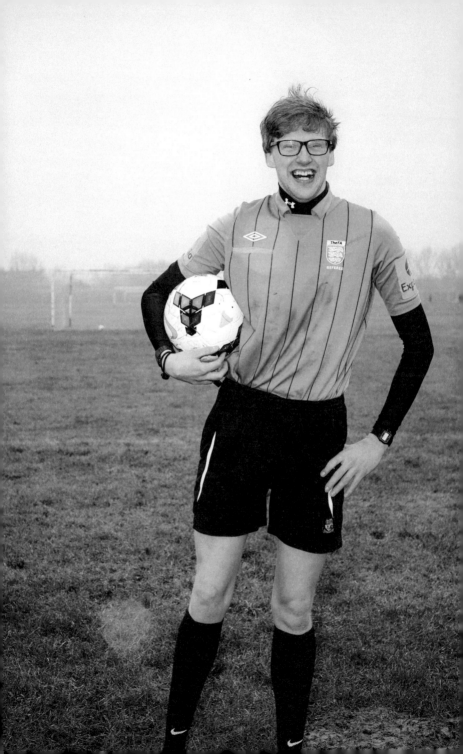

"No one wants to pull out due to being hungover, such things are heresy and usually lead to being dropped for a couple of weeks. Players' excuses include a car breakdown, an ill relative and, my personal favourite, which was pretending I was stuck in a lift. I even got out of bed and into my lift to add authenticity to the phone call."

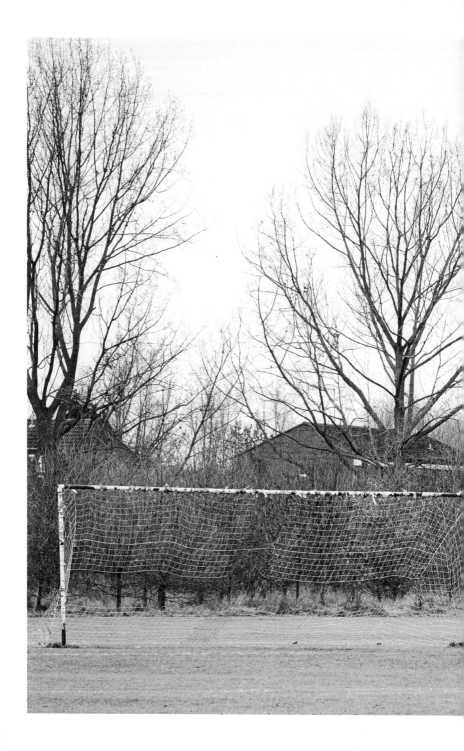

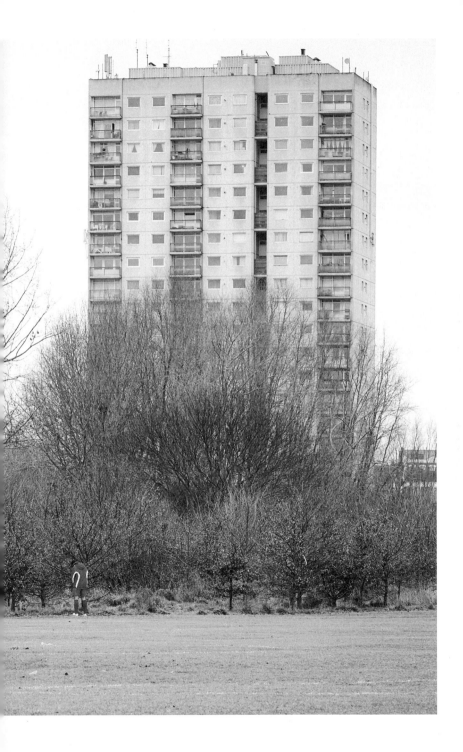

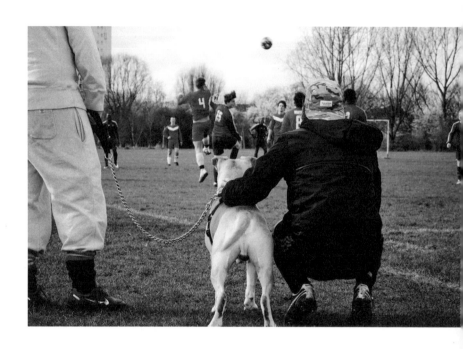

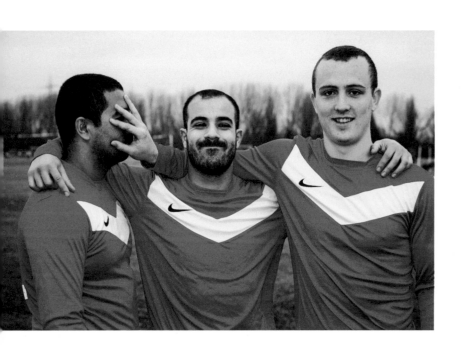

"Put your phone away,
we're playing football."

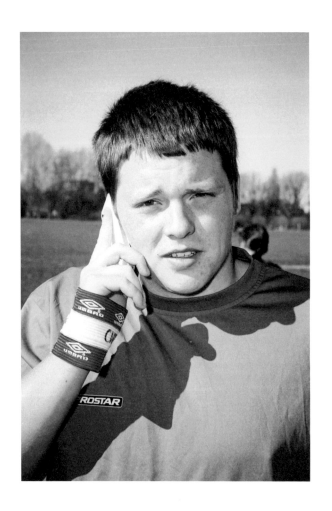

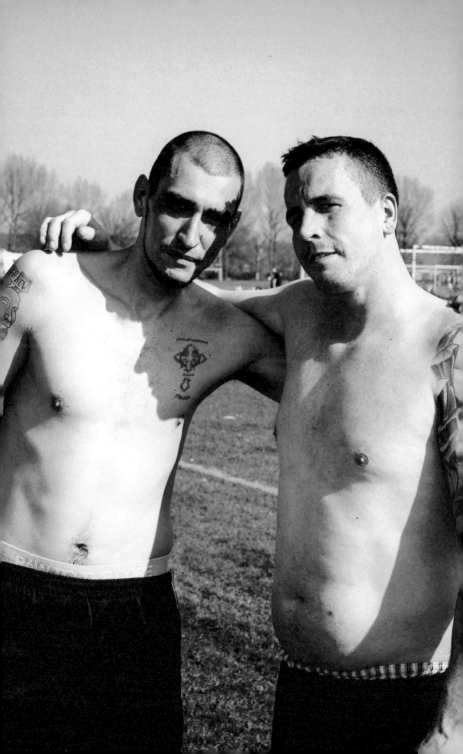

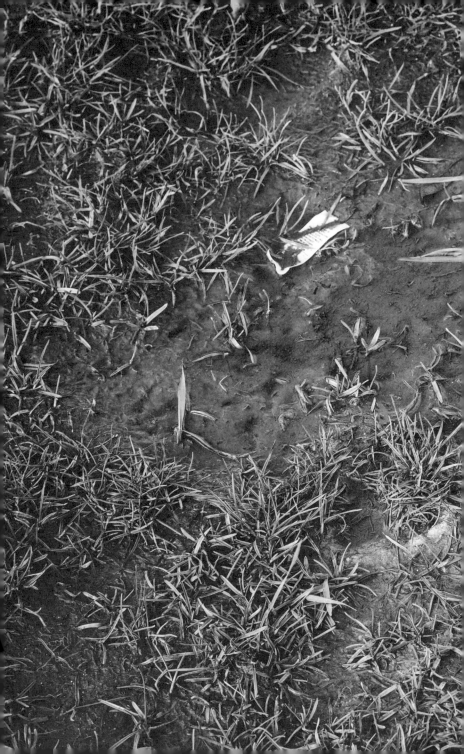

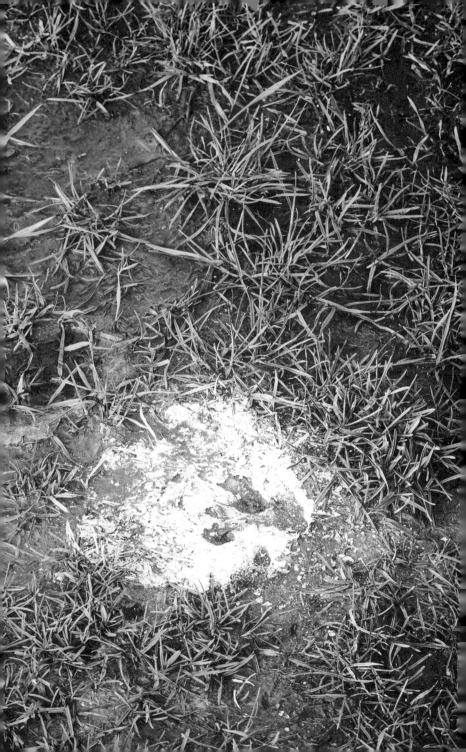

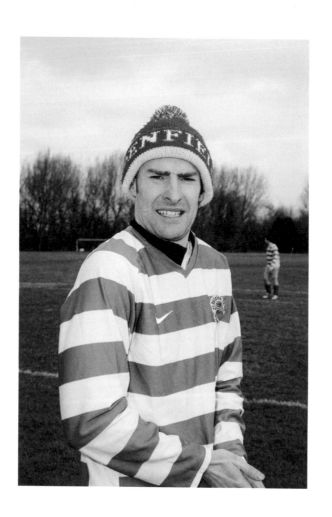

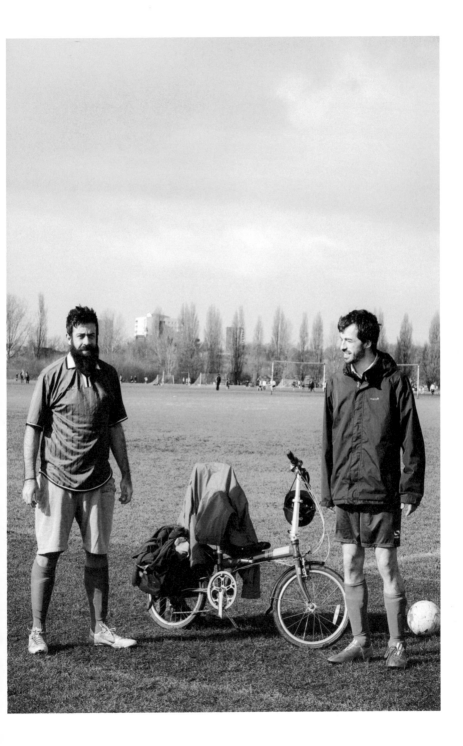

"As a striker I spend quite a bit of time on the halfway line next to the opposition centre-back as we defend corners.
I would normally never speak to this man. If we met in a pub we would walk past each other not acknowledging each other's existence. I would maybe check out his girlfriend in Topshop as he checks out mine. If he's a nice bloke he may ask how the season is going. If he's not, he will stare at me with a gaze colder than ice. 'Why are you talking to me?' This is war. He is the type of person I will look to eye-fuck when I score. Nothing is better than getting one over on an on-pitch nemesis. When the ninety minutes are up, our relevance to one another disappears. I'll keep an eye out for his missus next time I'm in H&M."

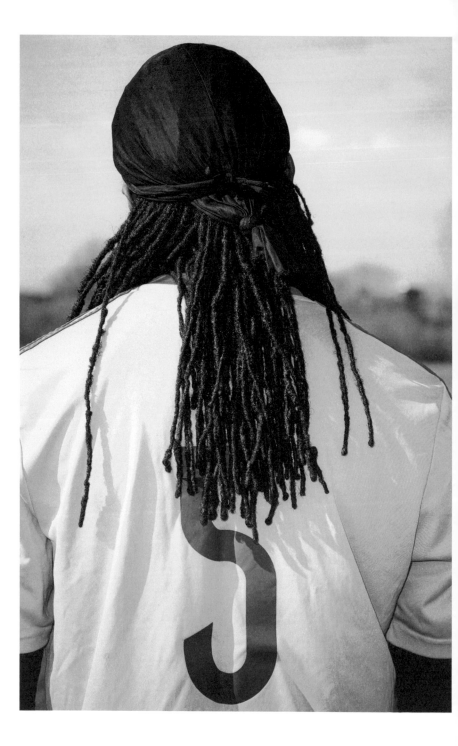

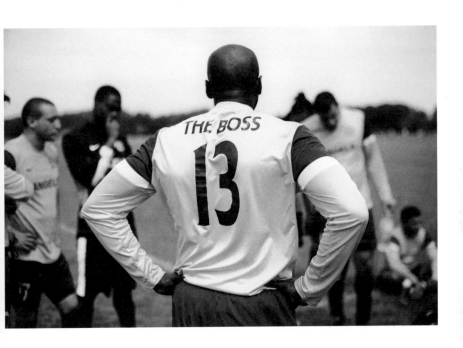

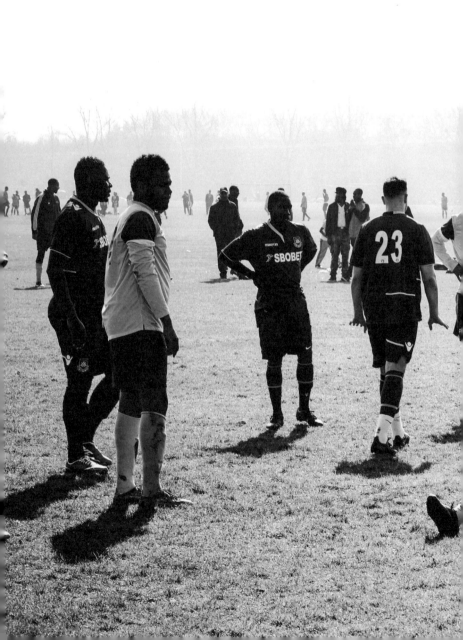

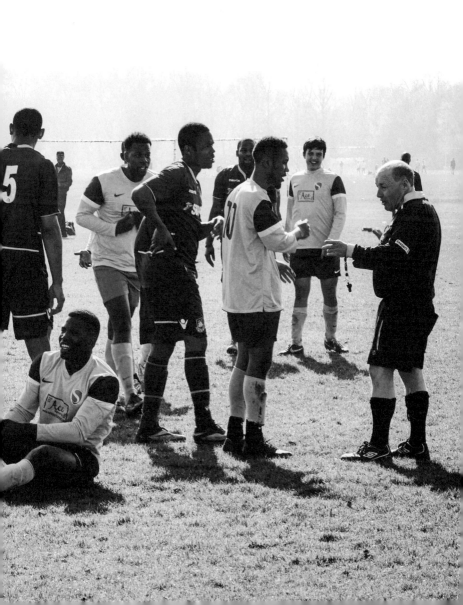

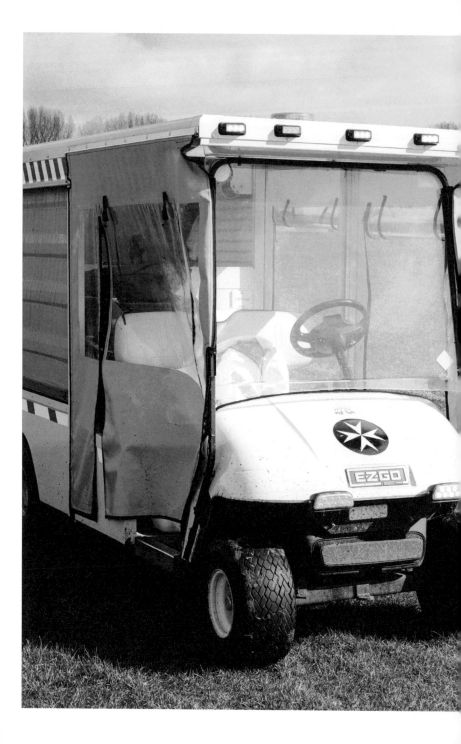

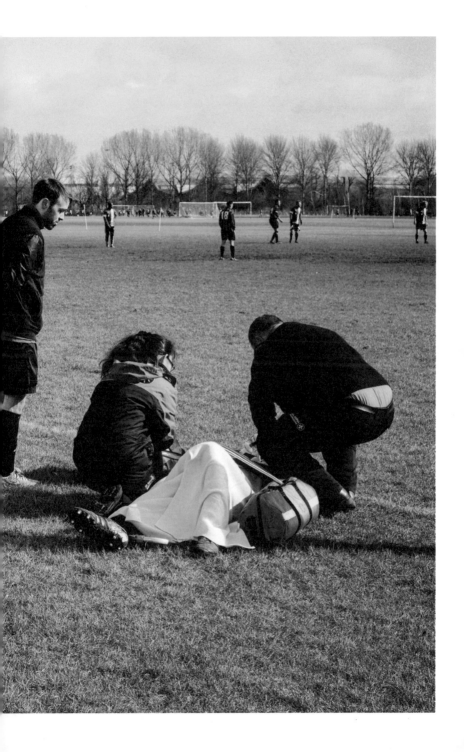

"Can you all just shut up?! Listen, there are too many people out there with egos wanting to be the leading goal scorer, that's fucking bollocks. We won't win like that, we'll only win if we play like a unit."

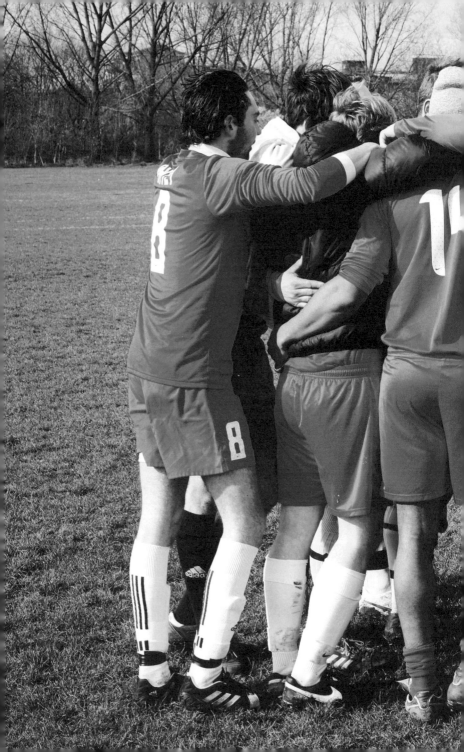

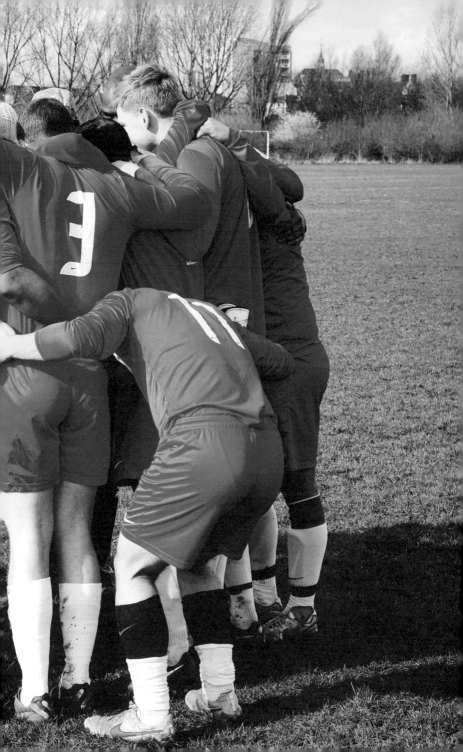

"He's our flashy striker. You should have seen what he had for breakfast: Eggs Benedict."

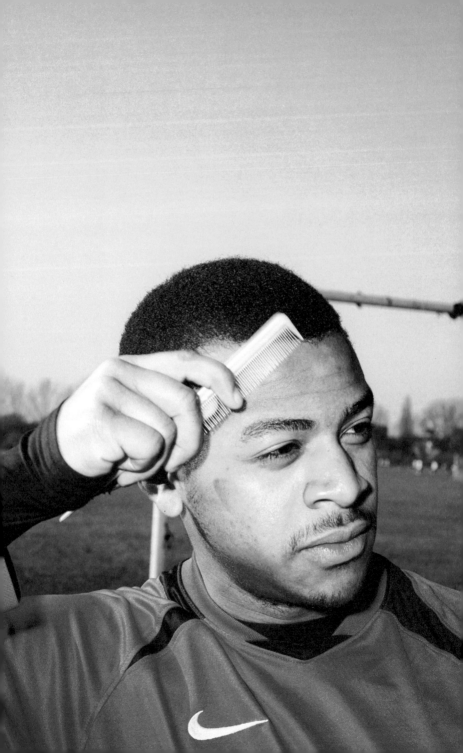

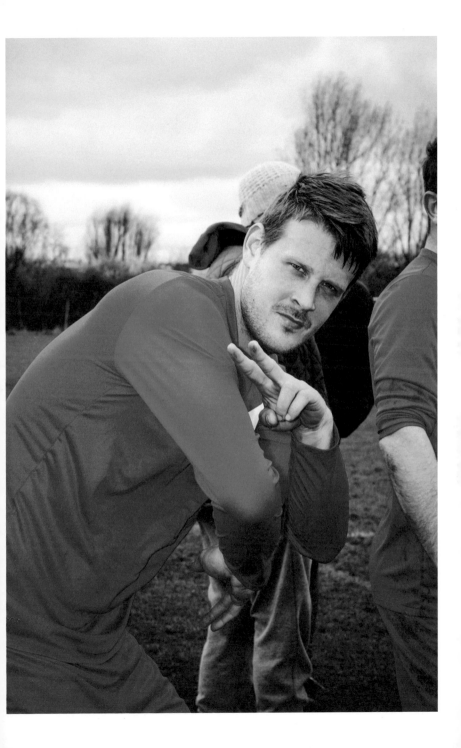

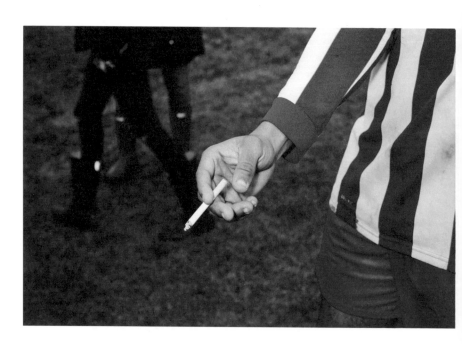

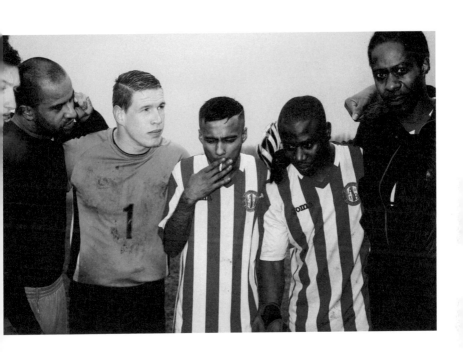

"It keeps me off the streets, something to do on a Sunday morning, although they try and discriminate against us because we like to puff and play football."

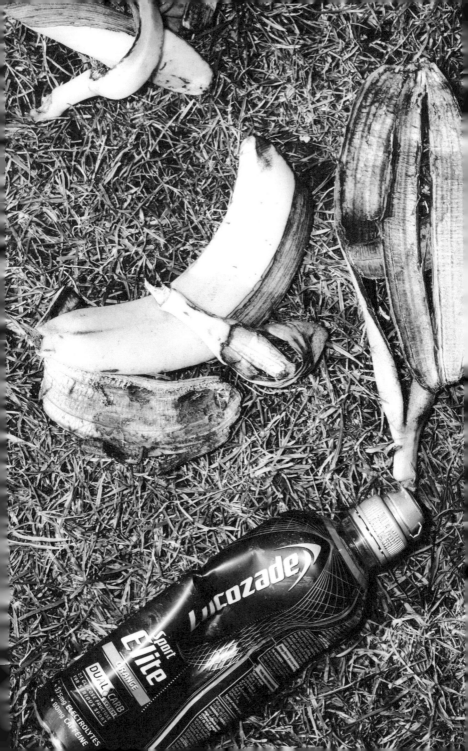

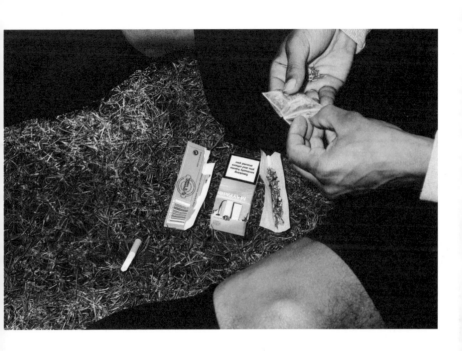

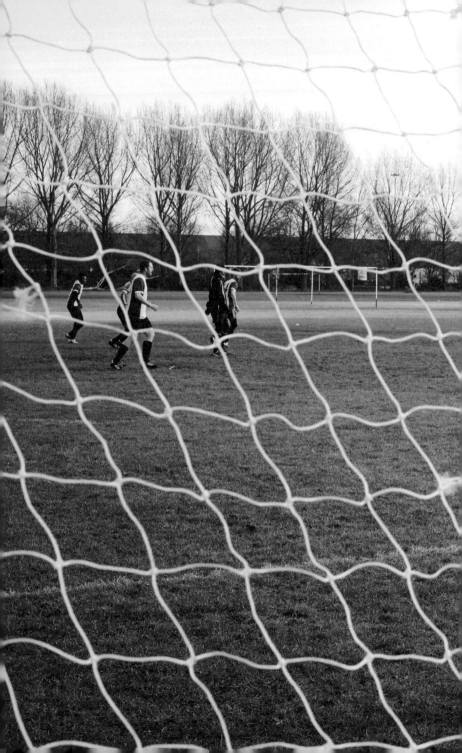

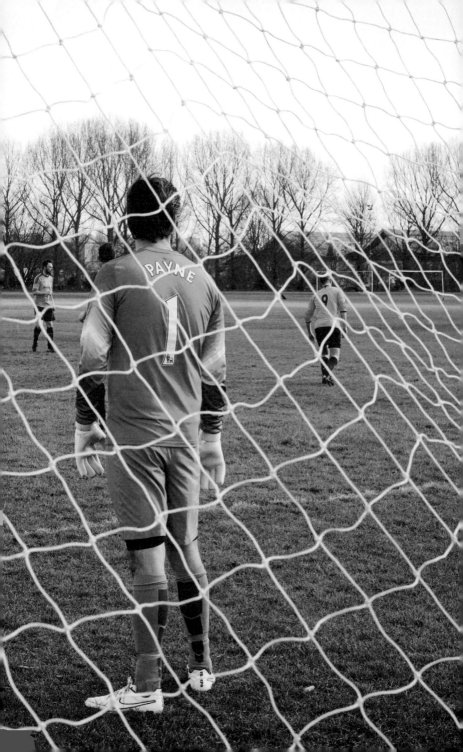

"Our old goalkeeper wore glasses but couldn't wear contacts. This was a bit of a problem as he could only really see a player or the ball when they reached the edge of his area. We conceded a lot of long-range shots that year."

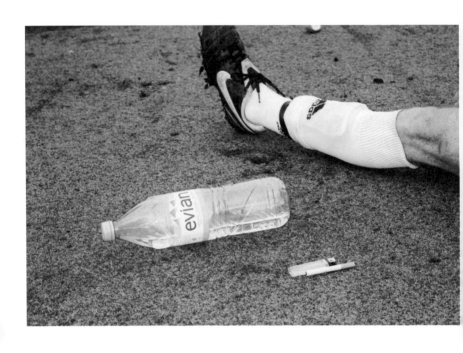

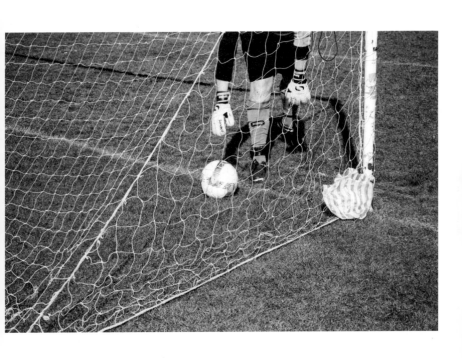

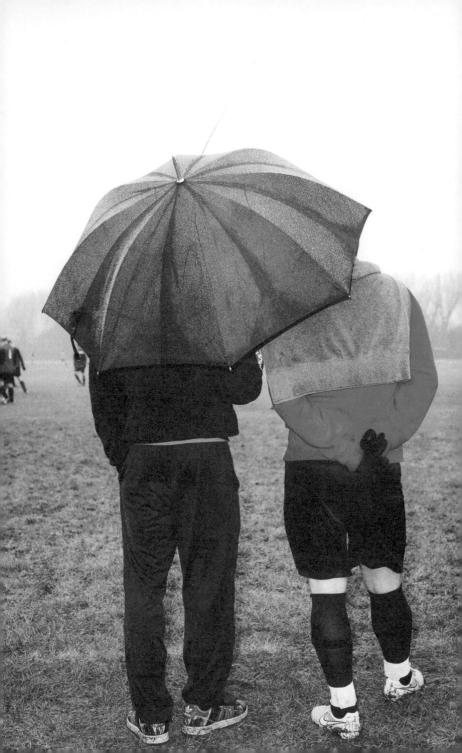

"One of the most important jobs of a Sunday morning football manager is being Taxi Driver. This usually means picking players up from various young ladies' houses or on the rare occasion, the local police station... all for free, I must add."

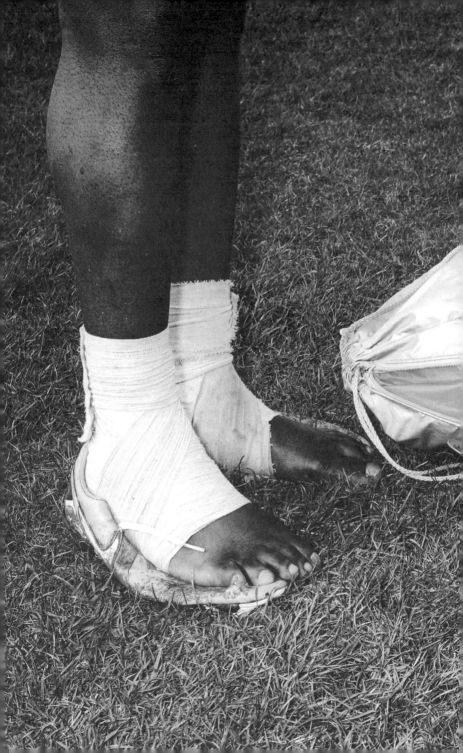

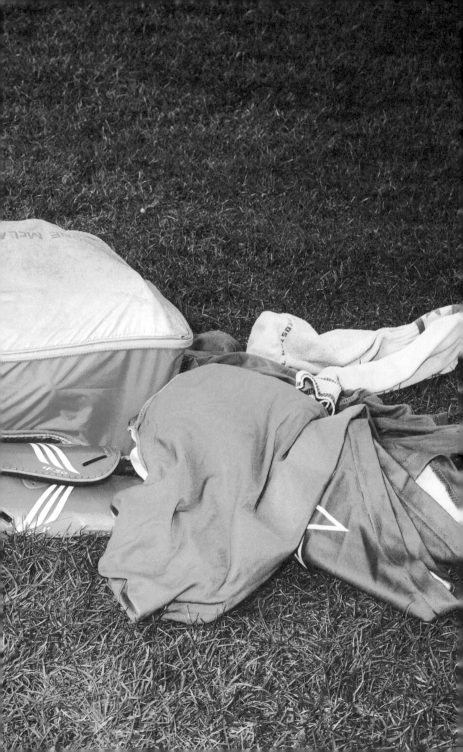

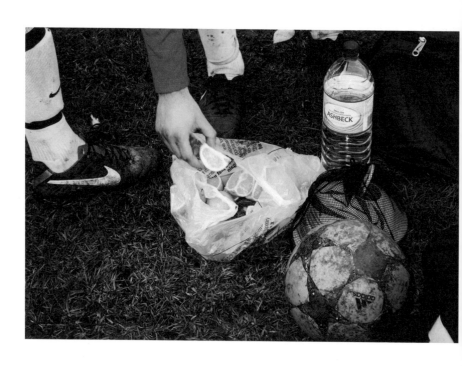

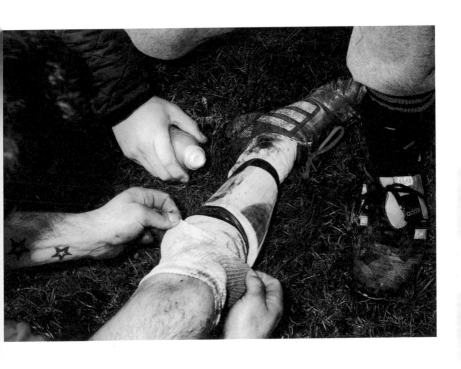

"My missus keeps asking why I can't play in black boots. She just doesn't get it, I *have* to wear yellow boots."

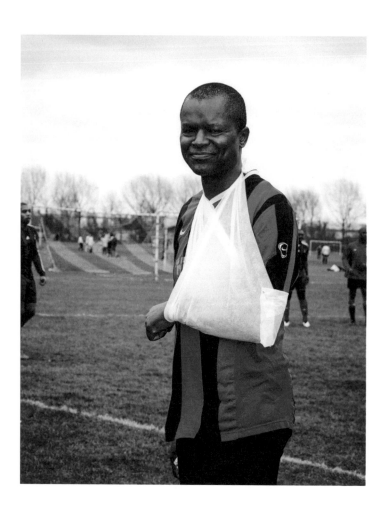

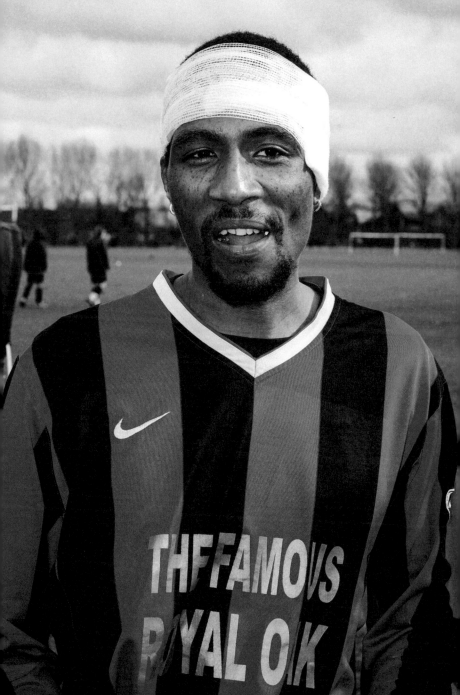

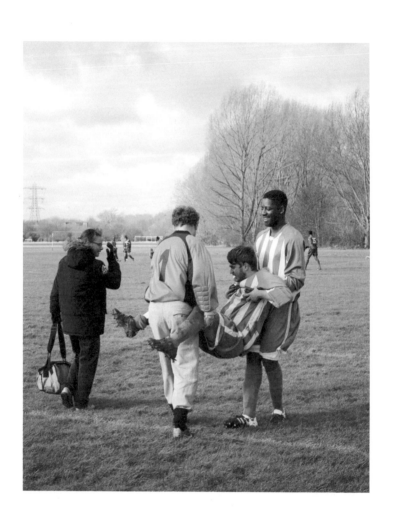

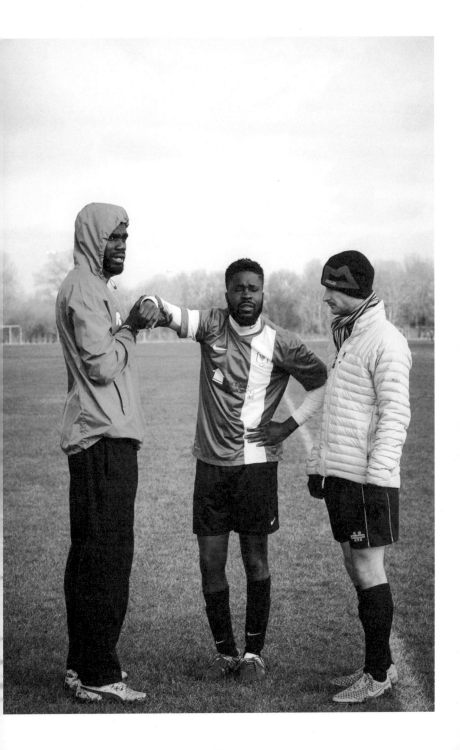

"Our keeper was in mid-air when the opposition striker kicked him so hard it broke his leg through the shin pad. When he landed from that he broke the ankle on the other foot. It's fucked his everyday life because he's got twin kids."

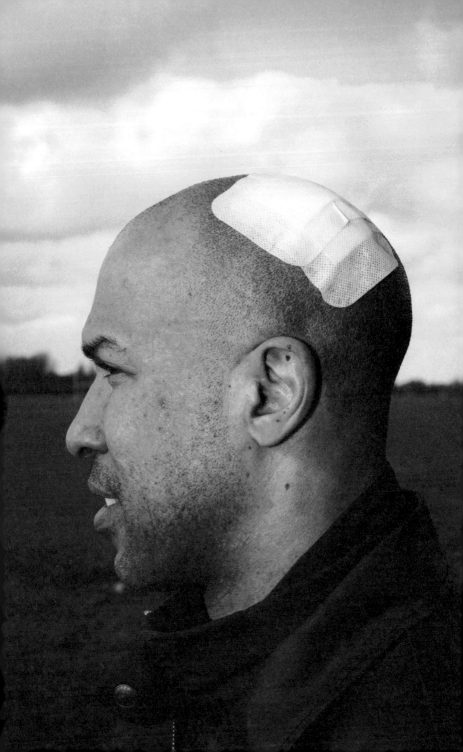

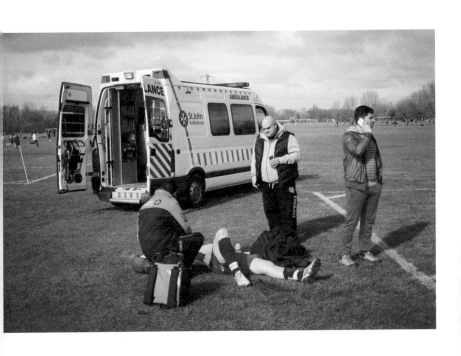

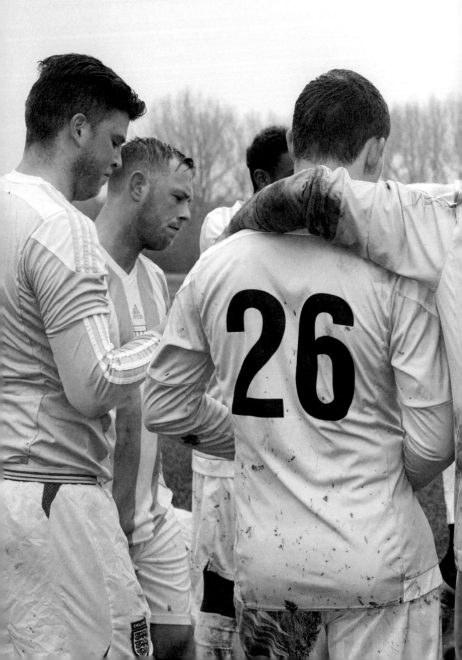

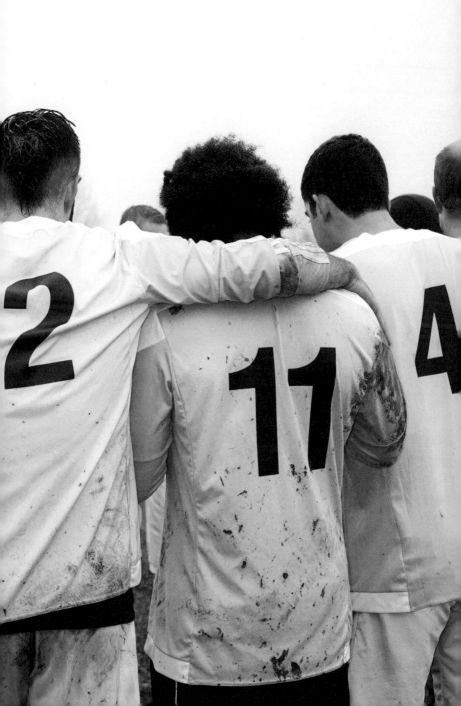

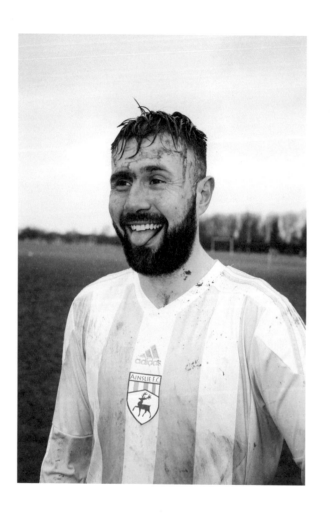

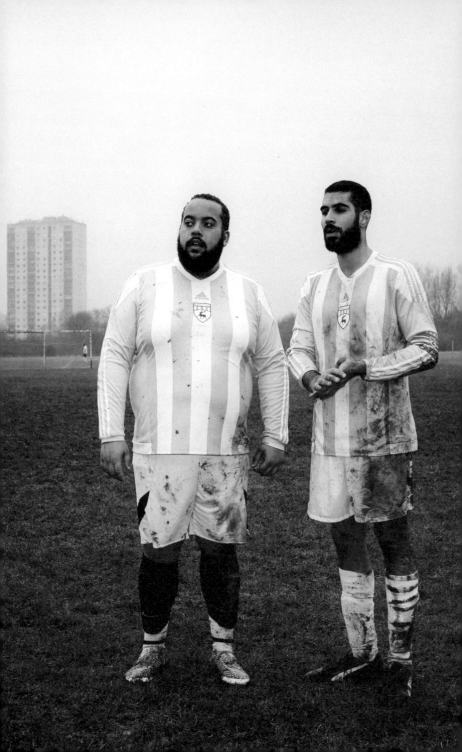

"One particular team had a reputation for trouble. They arrived at our grounds passing around a bottle of tequila. With a 10am kick-off they had decided to skip going home from the night before. The game had a lively start with tackles flying in, but it was all relatively good-humoured until we scored the first goal. Then it got really nasty. The ref lost control and we had double-footed tackles, punches and one of the subs exposing themselves to a player's wife. The police were called and some of their players received lifetime bans from the league."

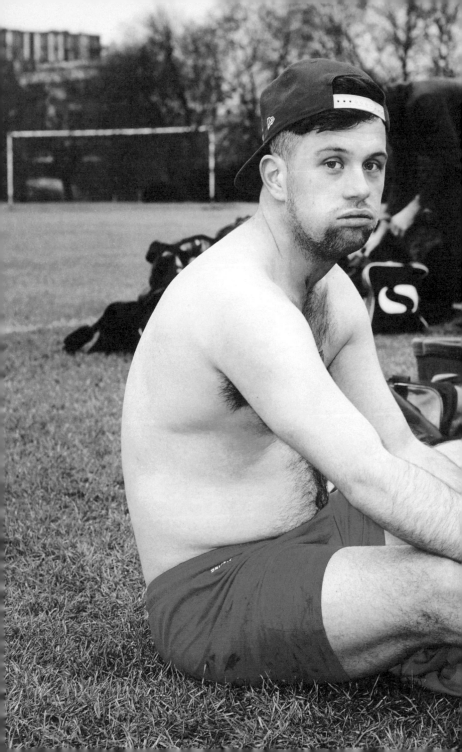

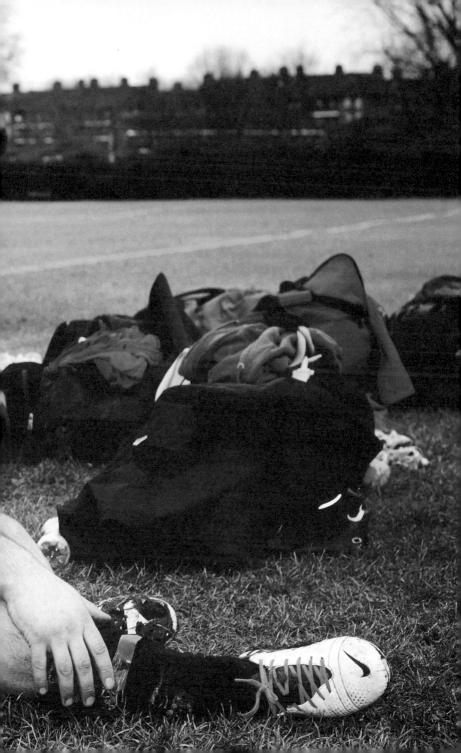

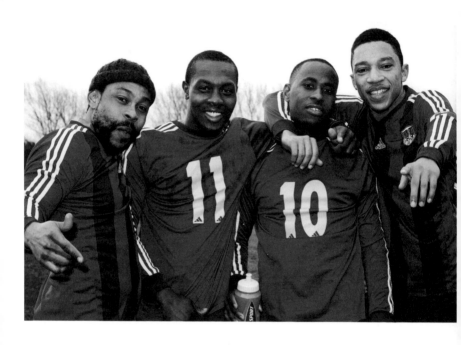

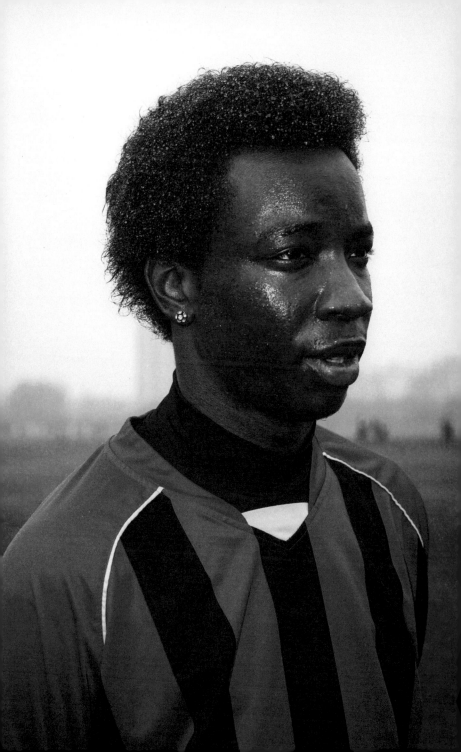

"My wife doesn't get it; this is where I come to see my mates."

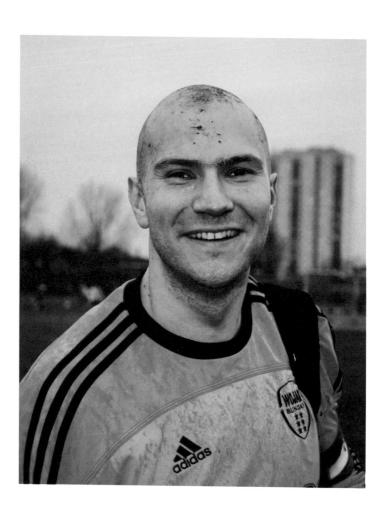

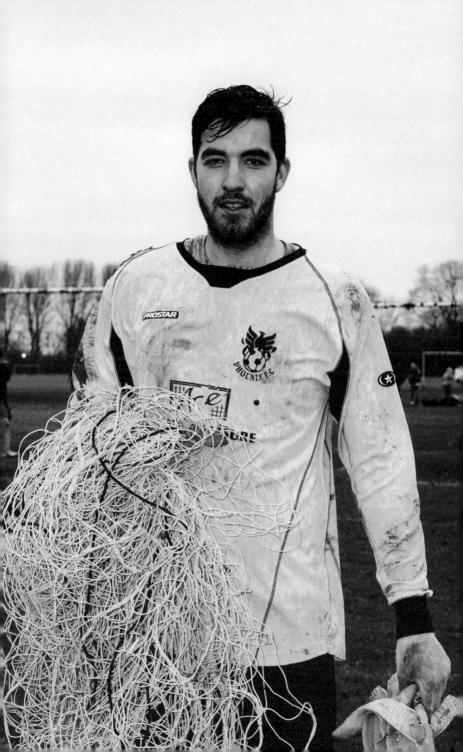

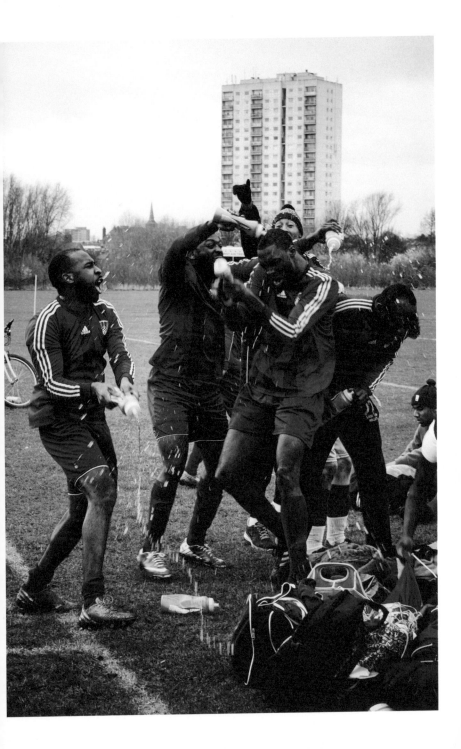

"If you play on a Sunday there's a real chance you've been on the sauce for at least one or two nights running. If I've been on the J-bombs the night before, the first forty five minutes are pure fire followed by a second half crash. More often than not the centre-half informs me he can smell the Red Bull seeping from my pores. This is classy and strikes fear into the opposition."

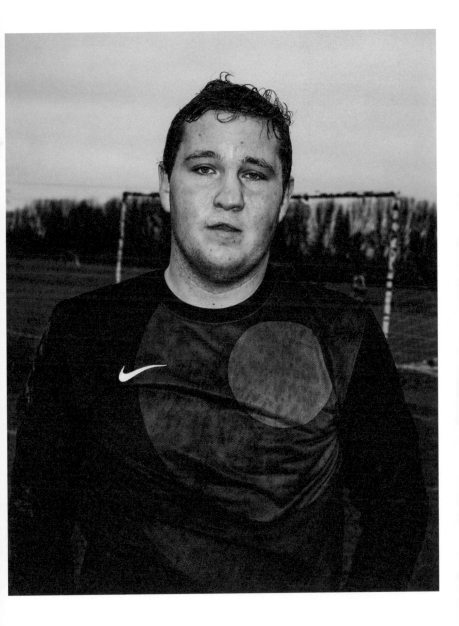

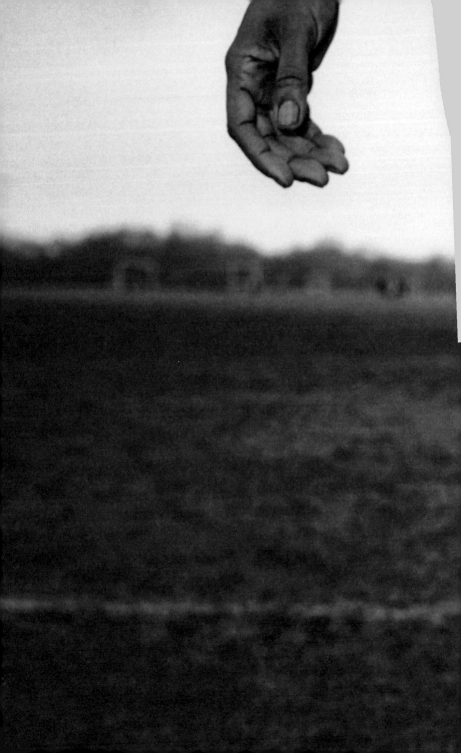

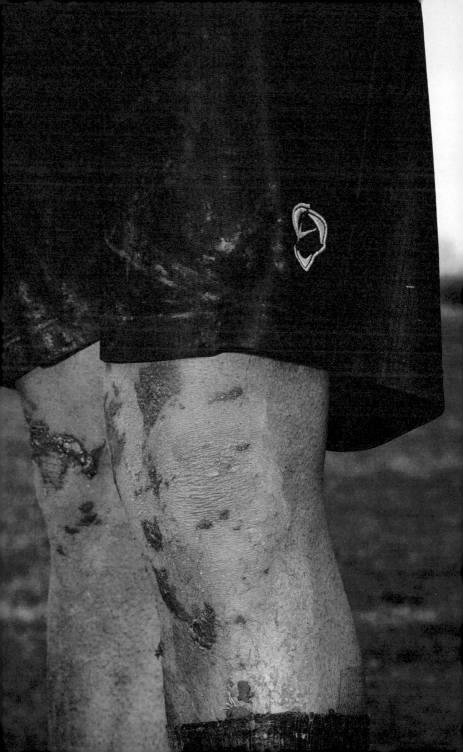

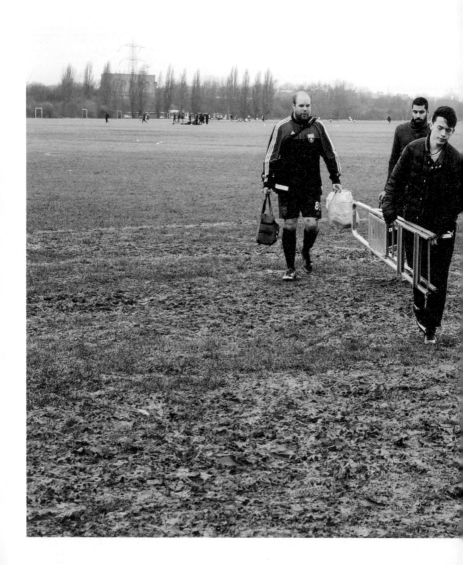

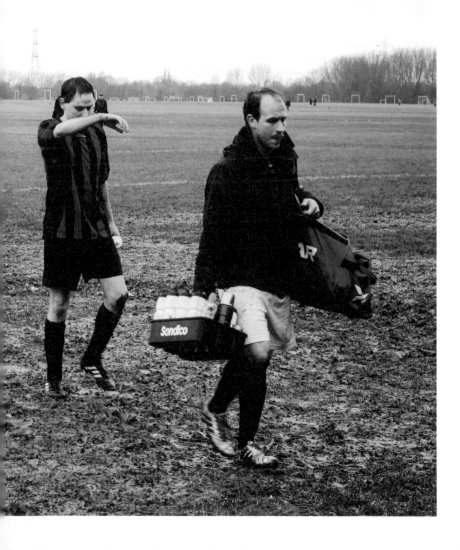

Sunday Football
First Edition

Copyright © Hoxton Mini Press 2016. All rights reserved.

All photographs © Chris Baker
Photo on page 10 credit: Bentley Archive/Popperfoto/Getty Images
Intro text by Chris Baker
Design and sequence by Friederike Huber, Chris Baker and Hoxton Mini Press
Series design by breadcollective.co.uk

A CIP catalogue record for this book is available from the British Library.

ISBN 978-1-910566-10-7

First published in the United Kingdom in 2016 by Hoxton Mini Press

Printed and bound by WKT, China on FSC®paper

To order books, collector's editions and signed prints please go to:
www.hoxtonminipress.com

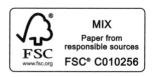